HEART to heart

A Discipleship and Mentoring Plan

Robin R. Ulbredtch

"Now hope does not disappoint, because the love of
God has been poured out in our hearts by the Holy
Spirit who was given to us."
(Romans 5:5 NKJV)

HEART to heart

A Discipleship and Mentoring Plan

Robin R. Ulbredtch

WestBow
PRESS
A DIVISION OF THOMAS NELSON

Scripture taken from the New King James Version. Copyright 1979, 1980, 1982 by Thomas Nelson, inc. Used by permission. All rights reserved.

Family and Author photographs by Steve Ulbredtch

WestBow Press books may be ordered through booksellers or by contacting:

WestBow Press
A Division of Thomas Nelson
1663 Liberty Drive
Bloomington, IN 47403
www.westbowpress.com
1-(866) 928-1240

ISBN: 978-1-4497-1764-3 (sc)

Library of Congress Control Number: 2011930025

Printed in the United States of America

WestBow Press rev. date: 7/12/2011

This book is dedicated to:

Jesus, my Savior and Lord, for paying the price for my sins, for saving me, and for all the wonderful things He has done, is doing, and will do in my life.

My family, especially my husband, Steve, for their patience and assistance in helping make this dream become a reality.

Pastor Wesley Ribeiro and the Elders, Deacons and their wives from Sandpoint Christian Center who counseled and encouraged me to step out and do what I believe God has asked me to do.

Leitha Harvey for believing in me, encouraging, helping, and standing beside me when I needed it the most. Thanks to Leitha for the many encouraging words she spoke that spurred me on to write. She is an excellent example of a Godly woman, and she has taught me many things! I hope someday that, like her, I can stand up, believe in, and spur someone else on like she has done for me. I hope I can be this kind of Godly example to others.

All the brothers and sisters in Christ who have encouraged and prayed for me over the years.

C. Max (Corky) and Gail Kalben for their encouragement and support over the years as I helped and interacted with them at the Bonner Gospel Mission.

Nils Rosdahl, Journalism Instructor at North Idaho College in Coeur d' Alene, Idaho, for taking his time and dedicating his life to teaching me and many other students how to write.

May God bless you all!

God's Infinite Love
By Robin Ulbredtch

I recently learned of a wonderful thing--
God's love for man, His created being.
God sacrificed His Only Son
so the souls of men might be won.

When we're born again and follow His rules,
God gives us treasure worth more than jewels.
He gives salvation to those who follow--
and keeps their lives from being hollow.

With salvation, when we believe--
God's precious gifts, we will receive.
He gives us guidance from above.
He fills our lives with His great love.

God gives us everything we need.
He'll guide us if, His Word we'll heed.
God forgives all our sin--
if we repent and ask Him in.

So do not worry and do not grieve--
in His hands, your burdens leave.
Pray for guidance from above,
and know His answer comes in love.

God always does what's best for us
If in Him, we'll put our trust.
For God's love was proven by His grace--
when He died on the cross to take our place.

So why not do it today?
Learn about Jesus and live life His way.
Then best of all, we'll have a friend
To travel with us to our journey's end.

So why not give Jesus a chance?
Why not ask Him to take our hand?
Why not belong to the Father above?
Why not experience God's infinite love?

CONTENTS

Preface   xi

Chapter 1   Introduction   1

Chapter 2   The Discipleship and Mentoring Plan   8

Chapter 3   Jesus is the Center   15

Chapter 4   The Team Meeting   17

Chapter 5   Small Discipleship Groups   25

Chapter 6   Church Authority and Leadership   28

Chapter 7   Choosing Group Leaders   30

Chapter 8   Choosing Discipleship Materials   32

Chapter 9   Bringing it all Together   34

Appendix A   37

Reproducibles   49

LIST OF FIGURES

Description:

HEART to heart Vision

HEART to heart Program Rules

Chain of Authority

Monthly Team Meeting Agenda

Ideas for Sharing Time- Women

Ideas for Sharing Time Classes-Women

Ideas for Sharing Time- Men

Ideas for Sharing Time Classes-Men

Reproducibles:

1. Letter of Inquiry (to find out if there is an interest in Discipling in your congregation)
2. Congregational Survey Form
3. Flyer
4. Membership List
5. Member Information Sheet
6. Team Meeting Member Attendance Chart
7. Communication Card

Preface

This HEART to heart plan is a tool created to encourage God's people to step out and share God's Word and the testimonies of His work in their lives with others to bring glory to God. We need to step out and give God the glory for what He has already done, what He is doing in our lives now, and what He promises He will do in the future.

While reading the book Women Mentoring Women[1] by Vickie Kraft and Gwynne Johnson (2003), I came across her idea of a program called HEART to heart where older and younger women gathered in small groups to fellowship, form friendships, and minister to one another's needs. As I read about this HEART to heart program I was encouraged about the women meeting together and growing in relationship with one another, but I sensed that something was missing. I couldn't figure out what was missing so I prayed.

Meanwhile, for several months, I believe God was speaking to me about starting a discipleship plan for people in our church. As I read about this HEART to heart program, God put the following verse in my mind and heart: "Now hope does not disappoint, because the love of God has been poured out in our hearts by the Holy Spirit who was given to us." (Romans 5:5 NKJV) Then I realized that their program was good for their purpose, but God wanted me to go another direction. He wanted me to put together the following HEART to heart Discipleship and Mentoring Plan.

I don't know of any better way to show the love of God to others than to teach His word to them, mentor them, and encourage them in their Christian walk. Many people are hurting in our churches and out in the world, and they need the love of God to change them and heal their hearts and lives.

With permission from Vickie Kraft, I used the name HEART to heart and a few ideas from *Women Mentoring Women*, but most of the structure and information came from my experience serving in Children's ministry programs, in a local men's mission and women's shelter, and from ministry I received while growing in my Christian faith.

The name HEART to heart was chosen because this plan is all about the work God is doing in the hearts of people. Only God has the power to change people, transform their lives, and give them hope for the future. Yet God has chosen to use His people as instruments to touch the lives of others and bring glory to His name.

God demonstrated His rich mercy and love by keeping me from taking my own life when I walked through a valley of despair due to circumstances in my life including the deaths of several family members within a short time span, the joy and nervousness of learning to care for a newborn infant, and the continual stress of being married to a man with an alcohol addiction.

I wanted to end my life to get away from the stress of the abuse and the hopelessness of living with someone who continued to drink in increasing quantities. I could see no hope for my future, and I wanted to get away from the pain of the abuse.

One day, when I was home alone with the baby, I believed some of the lies that Satan, the enemy of my soul kept telling me. "You are worthless! You don't contribute anything!"

After a time, I went into the kitchen and picked up a sharp steak knife and planned to cut my wrists with it. At the exact moment I held that knife up to my wrist and applied pressure to cut myself, my newborn son awoke from his nap and began crying loudly. I froze, and soon began thinking about what would happen to my son if I followed through with my plans. Then I realized I had to live for his sake, if no other reason. So I went to my son, picked him up from the crib, and sat down on the sofa trying to comfort him and calm myself down.

Suddenly, the Holy Spirit brought remembrance of past Bible lessons I had heard into my mind. The words "Jesus loves me" kept going through my mind, along with the stories of many of the miracles I heard Jesus had done. I learned about Jesus while attending a variety of churches during my school years. As I sat holding my son, suddenly I realized that God had stopped me from destroying myself because those words were really true! I knew God REALLY, TRULY loved me, and that He wanted me to live and take care of my son.

Since that time God has taken my broken heart and life and healed them. He has also used me in Children's ministry and a variety of other miscellaneous ways. Now, thirty years later, I look back at that day and realize the miracle that God worked in my life. I am still around to enjoy my new marriage, see my children grow up and have families of their own, and spend time with my grandchildren. I am also here to share the testimony of God's restoring work in my life with others. I am so thankful for all that God has done for me, and I know His miraculous healing power can transform and heal hearts and lives because He has done it for me.

Now my desire is to share God's word and the wonderful work he has done in my life with others because I know He can miraculously heal their hearts and lives too!

This HEART to heart Discipleship and Mentoring plan is a structured set of guidelines and ideas for anyone who desires to set up a discipleship and/or mentoring program in their local church, home, or other community place. It is designed to give believers a means of sharing what God has done for them with others to encourage them. It also provides an organized platform for teaching God's word, sharing gifts and talents, and helping others deal with the tough issues of life.

As Christian believers read through this book, I pray God will show each one how He can work through them to demonstrate His love and miraculous healing power to others in need. I pray that others will desire to teach God's word and begin a discipleship and mentoring group.

If this book can inspire one Christian believer to disciple and/or mentor another person in need, God will have used it to accomplish His great work.

God promises that His word will not come back void so I'm stepping out in faith to see what God will do with one small contribution from one of His children.

May God get the glory for all that is done!

Chapter 1

Introduction

Welcome to the HEART to heart Discipleship and Mentoring plan. It's my hope that this plan will encourage Christian believers to disciple and mentor one another with the Word of God and to share their testimonies about God work in their hearts and lives with others. God desires that we tell others about His unfailing grace, love, and mercy so that they can have their broken hearts and lives retored by His great healing power and they can become born again and become His adopted sons.

In the great commission, Jesus commanded us to do this. Matthew 28:18-20 NKJV[2] (Thomas Nelson, Inc. 2007) tells us about this commission saying, "And Jesus came and spoke to them, saying, 'All authority has been given to Me in heaven and on earth. Go therefore and make disciples of all the nations, baptizing them in the name of the Father and of the Son and of the Holy Spirit, teaching them to observe all things that I have commanded you; and lo, I am with you always, even to the end of the age.' Amen."

As you look at the cover for this program, notice that the first word "Heart" in the title of this book is capitalized because it speaks of the heart of God. God was in the beginning and He is the originator and source of great heart-changing power. God will change hearts and lives as this program is implemented, and will continue His work until He brings us to the end of His story, the great judgement recorded in the Biblical book of Revelation. God will bring judgement upon this earth and end His story when He determines the time has come for Him to finish His great work.

As Christians, we need to disciple others and share our testimonies with others. We need to comfort and encourage them—to spur them on to a close relationship with God and on to good works. We need to come along side of them and pray, and help them work through their difficulties. We need to share the love God pours into our hearts with those whom God brings into our lives.

In Genesis chapters one and two, we find God working, creating the heavens and the earth and all that is in it. We can read about God's creation of the plants, animals, birds, and fish and how He created each one according to its kind. After God has done this, He looks at His work and scripture tells us, "(…) And God saw that it was good." (Genesis 1:25 NKJV)

In this creation account we also see how God created man and woman in His image and likeness. Genesis 1:27 NKJV tells us, "So God created man in His own image; in the image of God He created Him; male and female He created them." God chose to make man and woman, and give them a purpose. In Genesis 1:28 it tells us part of God's purpose for our lives saying, "Then God blessed them, and God said to them, 'Be fruitful and multiply; fill the earth and subdue it; have dominion over the fish of the sea, over the birds of the air, and over every living thing that moves on the earth.'" God loved His created beings so much that He blessed them and gave them charge over all the living creatures.

Genesis 1:31 NKJV tells us about God's reaction to His creation saying, "Then God saw everything that He had made, and indeed it was very good" (…). God loved man and woman from the very beginning and that has not changed. John 3:16-17 NKJV tells us, "For God so loved the world that He gave His only begotten Son, that whoever believes in Him should not perish but have everlasting life. For God did not send His Son into the world to condemn the world, but that the world through Him might be saved."

Sometimes we get the mistaken idea that God is just waiting for us to make a mistake so He can discipline or punish us. We also have this idea of an impersonal God who doesn't care about us or our personal lives. Nothing can be farther from the truth! God is a personal, loving Father who is rich in mercy and abounding in love towards His created beings. God gave His Son to us to pay the penalty for our sins so that we could have salvation and eternal life. God made a way for us to come boldly before His throne in prayer and have a personal relationship with Him. God wants us to come to get to know Him, and the great love He has for us.

When referring to God's heart, we must know that it is love, in all of its various facets. Scripture tells us, "Beloved, let us love one another, for love is of God; and everyone who loves is born of God and knows God. He who does not love does not know God, for God is love." (1 John 4:7-8 NKJV)

God demonstrated His love for us and gave us an example of that love. Scripture tells us, "In this the love of God was manifested toward us, that God has sent His only begotten Son into the world, that we might live through Him. In this is love, not that we loved God, but that He loved us and sent His Son to be the propitiation for our sins." (1 John 4:9-10 NKJV)

Jesus, God's One and only Son, paid the penalty for our sins so that we might have eternal life and become adopted sons and members of His heavenly household. Scripture tells us, "Blessed be the God and Father of our Lord Jesus Christ, who has blessed us with every spiritual blessing in the heavenly places in Christ, just as He chose us in Him before the foundation of the world, that we should be holy and without blame before Him in love, having predestined us to adoptions as sons by Jesus Christ to Himself, according to the good pleasure of His will," (Ephesians 1:3-5 NKJV). God did this because He loves us. God's heart is love, and that love is for His Son and for us.

God wants a special people whom He can call His own, a people with whom He can fellowship, love, save, and bring into His kingdom to be His adopted sons. In Exodus 6:2-8 scripture tells us, "and God spoke to Moses and said to him: 'I am the Lord, I appeared to Abraham, to Isaac, and to Jacob, as God Almighty, but by my name Lord I was known to them. I have also established My covenant with them, to give them the land of Canaan, the land of their pilgrimage, in which they were strangers. And I have also heard the groaning of the children of Israel whom the Egyptians keep in bondage, and I have remembered My covenant. Therefore say to the children of Israel: 'I am the Lord; I will bring you out from under the burdens of the Egyptians, I will rescue you from their bondage, and I will redeem you with an outstretched arm and with great judgments. I will take you as My people, and I will be your God. Then you shall know that I am the Lord your God who brings you out from under the burdens of the Egyptians. And I will bring you into the land which I swore to give to Abraham, Isaac, and Jacob; and I will give it to you as a heritage: I am the Lord."

Paul's letter to Titus also speaks of God's desire for a special people as it says, "For the grace of God that brings salvation has appeared to all men, teaching us that, denying ungodliness and wordly lusts we should live soberly, righteously, and godly in the present age, looking for the blessed hope and glorious appearing of our great God and Savior Jesus Christ, who gave Himself for us, that He might redeem us from every lawless deed and purify for Himself His own special people, zealous for good works." (Titus 2:11-14 NKJV)

In 1 Peter 2:9-10 NKJV scripture tells us, "But you are a chosen generation, a royal priesthood, a holy nation, His own special people, that you may proclaim the praises of Him who called you out of darkness into His marvelous light; who once were not a people but are now the people of God, who had not obtained mercy but now have obtained mercy."

As we have seen from scripture, God desires and has a special people of His own to love and make up His heavenly household. God also wants His people to choose to love Him in return. God's heart is love--perfect, everlasting love.

In 1 Corinthians 13:1-13 NKJV scripture describes many facets of God's love. It also tells us about the value of that love saying, "And though I have the gift of prophesy, and understand all mysteries and all knowledge, and though I have all faith, so I could remove all mountains, but have not love, I am nothing." (1 Corinthians 13:2 NKJV) It goes on to say, "And now abide faith, hope, love, these three; but the greatest of these is love." (1Corinthians 13:13 NKJV) Yes, God's heart is everlasting, unfailing love.

As we come to the second 'heart' in the title of this HEART to heart discipleship and mentoring plan, we see the heart of mankind after they have been born again by God's Holy Spirit. We can see that God changes our sinful, unloving heart and gives us a new heart of flesh. In Ezekiel 11:16-20 NKJV God's messenger Ezekiel prophesies about the people of Israel saying, "Therefore say, 'Thus says the Lord God: 'Although I have cast them far off among the Gentiles, and although I have scattered them among the countries, yet I shall be a little sanctuary for them in the countries where they have gone.' Therefore say, 'Thus says the Lord God: 'I will gather you from the peoples, assemble you from the countries where you have been scattered, and I will give you the land of Israel.' And they will go there, and they will take away all its detestable things and all its abominations from there. Then I will give them one heart, and I will put a new spirit within them, and take the stony heart out of their flesh, and give them a heart of flesh, that they may walk in My statutes and keep My judgments and do them; and they shall be My people, and I will be their God."

Romans 5:5 NKJV says, "Now hope does not disappoint, because the love of God has been poured out in our hearts by the Holy Spirit who was given to us." Consequently, if we have been born again, God has poured His love into our hearts. Our hearts are the second hearts spoken of in this great plan of God's. He pours His love into our hearts so we can love Him back and love those around us. In fact, God gives us two commandments concerning this in Matthew 22: 34-40 NKJV which says, "Then one of them [Pharisees], a lawyer, asked Him a question, testing Him, and saying, 'Teacher, which is the great commandment in the law?'

Jesus said to him, 'You shall love the Lord your God with all your heart, with all your soul, and with all your mind. This is the first and great commandment.' And the second is like it: 'You shall love your neighbor as yourself. On these two commandments hang all the law and the prophets.'"

Loving God and loving others are two of the main goals of this 'HEART to heart' discipleship and mentoring plan. As God's people, we need to learn to love others not only in word, but with action. Love is not just a feeling. It is something we need to put into practice in our lives. None of us are perfect at loving, nor will we be perfect until God comes and changes us when He comes back to take us home with Him. Yet we should press on toward that goal.

Many of us have experienced the warm, wonderful side of love when we have met and married spouses or have children or other family members that are close to us. Yet how many of us realize that there is another side of love that is not so easy to accept? For example, one side of God's love is discipline, and God disciplines His people for their good. None of us like discipline, but it is necessary at times to keep us on the right path.

In addition, no one likes the idea of God's judgment or wrath coming into their lives, but at times God has to use these extreme measures to get our attention or for other reasons. God wants us to fix our eyes on Jesus, and keep them there so we can persevere through the many troubles that come our way during this life.

Thirdly, no one likes persecution or tests and trials, yet God allows them in our lives for His plan of transforming us into the image of His

Son. God allows these bad things to come into our lives in order to change us, strengthen us, break our stubborn will or for other purposes. In all these bad things we need to learn to persevere and trust God to work it all out. Romans 8:28 NKJV tells us, "And we know that all things work together for good to those who love God, to those who are the called according to His purpose."

Confrontation can also be a trial and a tool God uses to change us. At times confrontation is needed to work out difficulties in relationships or to change bad circumstances in our lives. Many of us hate confrontation and avoid it at all costs. Yet sometimes confronting others will let them know about problems that would have otherwise gone unresolved until someone got angry or hurt. Only recently God has shown me the importance of confronting the issues that bring trouble into our lives. As we learn to confront these problems and resolve the ones that can be resolved, we gain freedom.

God's allowing these bad things to come into our lives seems, on the surface, to be unloving. Yet this is a 'tough' side of love that produces good things in our lives. As we mature in Christ, we need to learn to trust Him more even during these bad times.

You may be thinking that "This is easy for you to say but not so easy to do."

I agree, and in telling you to trust God during the tough times, I'm not trying to say that it's easy for us to do. Difficult circumstances can shake our faith to the core and cause us to doubt God. During these times, we need to draw closer to Him and to enlist the help of our caring brothers and sisters in Christ for encouragement, love, and support. This HEART to heart plan could open the door and provide a place for people to go and get the encouragement, love, and support of God's family during the tough times.

Reaching out to others and helping them through "tough times" is one example of mentoring. A second example of mentoring could be teaching others the life skills needed to fulfill the role God has given them during our pilgrimage on this earth. Some of these skills can include cooking, sewing, money management, reading, language, mathematics, menu planning, shopping, needlecrafts, budgeting, home repair, car maintenance, parenting, and the list continues on ... Teaching others these life skills helps them to improve their quality of life. Mentoring others in this way can be a means of reaching out with the love God has given us. When we reach out to others in this way, God uses us to touch their hearts, and He works through us to meet their needs. Then God gets the glory for what He has done!

Discipleship is following Jesus and teaching others to do the same. It involves reading God's word, teaching it to others, and sharing with them the wonderful things God has done in our lives. It means encouraging, sharing our gifts and talents, and fellowshipping with others, whether it be one-on-one or with a large group of people. Jesus had a core group of twelve disciples who followed Him and learned from His way of life.

As we endeavor to implement this 'HEART to heart discipleship and mentoring plan' into the lives of those around us, we need to seek God and ask Him to give us everything we need to help those He brings into our lives. We need to have times of fellowship and sharing where we can encourage and pray for one another.

James gives us good advice saying, "If any of you lacks wisdom, let him ask of God; who gives to all liberally and without reproach, and it will be given to him. But let him ask in faith, with no doubting, for he who doubts is like a wave of the sea driven and tossed by the wind. For let not that man suppose that he will receive anything from the Lord; he is a double-minded man, unstable in all his ways." (James 1:5-7 NKJV)

We don't want to be like that wave. We want to be stable and steadfast in our walk with the Lord. A discipleship and mentoring plan can bring Christian believers together to love and support one another, to learn about the word of God, and to help us become more mature in the faith and more like Jesus. It can also provide a place where unbelievers can come to see the love of God in action and possibly give their lives to Jesus. So let's move ahead to the next chapter and see the details of this plan.

Chapter 2

The Discipleship and Mentoring Plan

This HEART to heart Discipleship and Mentoring plan consists of basically five components: (1) Jesus, the center and foundation, (2) a regular Team meeting, (3) individual discipleship groups of two or more people, (4) your church authority and leadership and (5) the materials your church chooses to use for discipling others. With these components, and everyone committed and under submission to Jesus Christ, the Discipleship and Mentoring Plan should flourish.

Jesus Christ is now and will always be the center and foundation of a true discipleship plan. We should all endeavor to follow Jesus, and become His disciples. We will learn more about disciples and discipleship in the training materials chosen by the church leadership to use for fulfilling this plan. We should all look to Jesus Christ as our Lord and Savior, endeavor to do His will, and pursue an individual relationship with Him. We need to stay plugged in to the source of life!

As the challenges of the end times come upon us, we will need to stand together and support each other even more than we do already. Other people, possibly the lost or poor, will need a place to come for discipleship, mentoring, and help in dealing with the tough issues of life. Endeavor to make your HEART to heart group a place where people can come and get pointed toward—and plugged into—Jesus, the source of life.

The second component of this plan is a regular Team Meeting. This meeting will be put on once or twice a month for the purpose of inspiring and supporting the smaller discipleship groups, and for mentoring. This meeting will endeavor to provide a platform for encouragement, fellowship, prayer, worship, training in Discipleship, answering questions, sharing of gifts and other things that will edify one another, referring people who have needs to resources that may help meet those needs, mentoring, and dealing with any issues (good or bad) that may come up during the discipleship groups or team meetings.

The third component of this Discipleship and Mentoring Plan is the small discipleship groups. These groups can be held in a church, a home, or in a place in the community. This group setting is where most of the discipleship and mentoring will take place. People should come together every week to study the word of God together. As they come, they should be prepared to learn about God and the wonderful things He does. They should be free to ask questions and share personal conversation with others in the group. Each group can choose a time and meeting place that works best for them. If possible, childcare should be provided during the small group meetings for women who may have young children.

As I believe the Lord has brought people into my life for me to disciple, I believe He will bring together discipleship groups as the people meet and get to know each other. In fact, the Lord may have already put together some small groups of people who study the Bible together. Perhaps these groups would like to join the discipleship and mentoring program and draw from the resources it provides. Endeavor to support them as they already exist and add new people as the program grows.

The fourth component of this discipleship and mentoring plan is the church authority and leadership. These leaders are probably already in established in the church, and they should get honor and respect. They are established by God to help the people of the congregation deal with any issues, scriptural or otherwise, that may cause danger to the congregation. They are watchmen over the congregation and they have Godly wisdom. If the HEART to heart groups need to seek Godly counsel and guidance, they should go to their church leaders.

Every disciple needs to learn to submit to the church leaders, and trust that they will do their best to help. If you encounter a church leader who is unwilling to help by answering questions or referring you to someone else that can help you, pray for that person. Church leaders are meant to be God's servants and to oversee the church congregation and help keep order and peace.

If possible, encourage or enlist the church leadership to get involved in the discipleship and mentoring program. I believe having the church leadership involved is a blessing, and it helps insure that everything stays on the right path. After all that's another reason why God gave us our leaders!

The last component of the HEART to heart discipleship and mentoring plan is the Bible and/or Bible-teaching materials used in the small groups. The materials can come from a wide range of resources available in the Christian Bookstores or on the Internet. It isn't necessary to spend a large amount of money for these materials. Each person attending the group should pay for their own study book unless other arrangements have been made. More information on materials can be found in the chapter on Bible teaching materials.

On the following pages you will find a suggested "vision" for the HEART to heart Discipleship and Mentoring Program. Any church desiring to use this vision can, if needed, make changes so it will work for them. I pray that any changes will be in agreement with God's word. It's vital that this Discipleship program keeps Jesus as the center and the one being followed.

The Holy Spirit will help us learn about Jesus as we study God's word.

HEART to heart Vision:

1. To Love the Lord with all of our heart--corporately and individually.
2. To Love our neighbor as ourselves with the love God has poured into us by His Holy Spirit—corporately and individually.
3. To design and implement a Discipleship Program that helps equip the saints by:
    A. Pointing them to Jesus and teaching them the Word of God.
    B. Training them for works of service.
    C. Training them how to be a disciple.
    D. Training them how to disciple others.
    E. Overseeing those who are disciples in the program.
    F. Providing times of fellowship and worship.

G. Providing times where they can share their gifts and talents.

H. Providing times where they can share praise reports and testimonies.

I. Providing encouragement and support during difficult times.

J. Providing someone to whom they can go for prayer.

K. Teaching and supporting them a variety of information and ideas they can use to help them in their daily living.

L. Encouraging them to allow, embrace, and whenever possible, understand the changes God wants to make in their heart and lives.

M. Providing support for conflict resolution.

N. Equipping and preparing the saints for work in Evangelism, Discipleship, Teaching, Pastoral ministry and Apostle/Missionary work by teaching them from God's word.

4. To do what we can to encourage and provide support for people when they have needs that must be addressed, and to help them work through problems in their lives. We do not provide professional counseling services, but can refer people to the Pastor and other community resources for the help they need.

5. To provide a platform where people can feel free to share their challenges and possibly get ideas to help them find a solution. We want to encourage members to deal with their problems rather than stuffing them inside and hoping they will go away. To help people see their choices, and the consequences of each choice.

6. To provide a platform where people can demonstrate, through application, their love for God and others through various works of service.

7. To provide a platform where older saints can disciple and mentor younger ones, and where younger saints can get encouragement, hope and love from those who have been through experiences similar to the ones they face.

8. To provide a platform where group members can bring the lost to get a demonstration of God's love in action and possibly become born again.

9. To provide a platform where Christian people can have opportunity to do works of service for others in the church or in the community.

Along with the HEART to heart vision, I have made a set of rules for the groups to help establish guidelines. Each church can alter these rules as they see fit if needed. Rules are an important part of keeping peace and order when people get together. Without rules we leave the door open for Satan to come in and create chaos and conflict within the group. We want to avoid this as much as possible. The HEART to heart rules appear on the following page.

HEART to heart Program Rules:

1. People must be age 16 or above to participate in the program because some of the material brought out in team and small group meetings may not be appropriate for small children. (i. e. personal testimony)
2. People who are group leaders must be age 18 or above, born again, knowledgeable about scripture, in agreement with the church Statement of Faith, and be approved by the leadership in order to be able to disciple others.
3. Any private information shared in the group meetings or during discipleship meetings must be kept confidential except for when someone may be in danger. If you suspect someone is in serious trouble, please contact a pastor, elder, Team Leader or the appropriate emergency and/or law enforcement people.
4. We love your children. However, young children may not be present at the meetings because some content from the meetings may not be appropriate for them to hear. However, we will attempt to provide childcare during meeting times. Children can also create distractions during teachings, classes, and mentoring times and hinder personal-Sharing Time. We need to focus on the teachings and conversations. We also need to respect those doing the teachings, presentations, and sharing their personal situations by not interrupting and by listening to what they have to say.
5. We need to respect and love each person in the group. All personal arguments and issues between members must be handled privately in mediation or left outside the door when you come in. If you are in need of mediation, please contact the Team Leader or arrange a meeting with a pastor or leader to help work out a solution. We have an extremely low tolerance for arguing, fighting or worse during meeting times.
6. We are there to encourage and support one another. We also have an extremely low tolerance for any "putting down" or "criticizing" of others in the group meetings. We all have our own personal issues that need worked on. We need to work on getting the log out of our own eye first. If we do that, we

won't have time for criticizing others. Anyone caught tearing others down will be given three warnings. If the behavior doesn't stop, they will be asked to leave the meeting. They may return to the following meeting provided they keep their tongue in check.

7. We ask that everyone be sensitive to the fact that others may want to speak and/or ask questions. We do want to address your questions and hear your comments, but please don't take up long periods of time with visiting or sharing of stories that don't really apply. Someone else may need serious help, and if they can't get a word in, they may not get the help they need.

8. Serious problems that may arise during the meetings may be referred to the pastor or elders for discipline and/or resolution. Since this ministry is a part of the body of Christ, these matters may be directed to the church authorities who were put in place by God to deal with them.

In addition to the HEART to heart vision and rules, I have made some forms to help organize your Discipleship and Mentoring groups. You can find these forms in Appendix A in the back of this book. Feel free to copy these forms or make your own.

In scripture, Jesus tells us, "For where two or three are gathered together in My name, I am there in the midst of them." (Matthew 18:20 NKJV) I believe as Christians come together, God will meet with them and make this HEART to heart Discipleship and Mentoring Program a blessing to everyone involved.

Chapter 3

Jesus is the Center

In this HEART to heart Discipleship and Mentoring program, Jesus is the center—it all revolves around Him. God sent Jesus into the world to save men and women from their sins. Jesus died on the cross to pay the penalty for our sins. Three days later, He rose from the dead and made a way for us to get to heaven. Jesus now sits and the right hand of the Father and intercedes for the children of God as they make their way down the narrow path toward heaven.

In Hebrews 2:5-12 NKJV scripture tells us, "For He has not put the world to come, of which we speak, in subjection to angels. But one testified in a certain place, saying, 'What is man that You are mindful of him, or the son of man that You take care of Him? You have made Him a little lower than the angels; You have crowned Him with glory and honor, and set Him over the works of Your hands. You have put all things in subjection under His feet.' For in that He put all in subjection under Him, He left nothing that is not put under Him. But now we do not yet see all things put under Him. But we see Jesus, who was made a little lower than the angels, for the suffering of death, crowned with glory and honor, that He, by the grace of God might taste death for everyone.

Jesus died on the cross and gave His all for us. Therefore, we need to center our lives around Him and the work He accomplished on the cross at Calvary. He is our example of love and the author of our faith. How can we do anything with out Him? He is the reason that we exist and have life.

He is the way for us to enter God's promise and become an adopted son in God's heavenly household.

For it was fitting for Him, for whom are all things and by whom are all things, in bringing many sons to glory, to make the captain of their salvation perfect through sufferings. For both He who sanctifies and those who are being sanctified are all of one, for which reason He is not ashamed to call them brethren, saying, 'I will declare Your name to My brethren; In the midst of the assembly I will sing praise to You.' And again: 'I will put My trust in Him.' And again: 'Here am I and the children whom God has given Me.'" God has given Jesus all authority over all the works of His hand, including you and me.

We should give Him all the pleasure and glory we can!

Chapter 4

The Team Meeting

The monthly team meeting vision is to create a warm, friendly environment for all the HEART to heart discipleship and mentoring groups to gather, fellowship, worship, and teach and mentor one another.

Each HEART to heart Discipleship and Mentoring program should have a Team Leader in place to oversee the program. This Team Leader, if desired, can enlist others to help him/her oversee the group. The size of the whole team will determine the number of leaders and types of leadership needed.

The Team Meeting is the place where the Team Leader and her helpers work to mentor, teach, and provide oversight for each of the groups. For example, if a small group leader encounters a question in scripture that he or she cannot answer, they can go to the Team Leader or the leader's helpers to get the information needed. This will provide a buffer for the leadership so they will not be overloaded with work. Also, small group leaders who come across members of their group with natural or spiritual needs can come to the Team Leadership for possible referrals as to where to go to get the need met. The team meeting should be a place where the people can feel the freedom to fellowship and share their heart with others. It should be a place where they can find the love of Jesus is action and where they can feel comfortable enough to bring a friend or family member along with them.

As you continue your disciple and mentoring group, make it an intimate time of training and ministering to the needs of those around you. In this world darkness abounds and an increasing number of people will need encouragement and support to deal with life. Make this group a light that reaches out to your community with the love that God pours into your hearts.

Also, make your group a safe shelter for those who drastically need a refuge and to come to know the living God. Nothing will draw people in more than seeing the love of God demonstrated before their very eyes. In scripture it tells us, "The Lord builds up Jerusalem; He gathers together the outcasts of Israel. He heals the broken hearted and binds up their wounds." (Psalm 147:2-3 NKJV) Scripture also tells us, "The Spirit of the Lord God is upon Me, because the Lord has anointed Me to preach good tidings to the poor; He has sent Me to heal the brokenhearted, to proclaim liberty to the captives, and the opening of the prison to those who are bound; to proclaim the acceptable year of the Lord, and the day of vengeance of our God; to comfort all who mourn, to console those who mourn in Zion, to give them beauty for ashes, the oil of joy for mourning, the garment of praise for the spirit of heaviness; that they may be called trees of righteousness, the planting of the Lord, that He may be glorified." (Isaiah 61:1-3 NKJV) Let us and these discipleship and mentoring groups be the vessels God can use to accomplish this great work! With God, all things are possible.

For the Team meetings, it's important to group men together in one group and women in another. This will provide a platform where the people can share their personal issues without fearing that someone of the opposite gender will be embarrised or put on the spot. Personal issues need to be shared with those of the same gender who have possibly gone through the same experience and can understand the emotions and feelings that go along with the experience. Because God made men and women to be different from each other, they sometimes struggle to relate with one another. It's important for everyone to feel safe in sharing with the group.

Any issues or questions that arise in the small groups that cannot be answered within the group should be brought to the Team Meeting. If the issues are personal or private matters, they should be directed to the HEART to heart Team Leader. If the leader cannot answer the issues, they can pray with you and direct you to the Lord or Godly counsel. Personal, private issues should be handled with the utmost care, and private information should not be shared outside of the small group unless that individual decides to seek advice or to share information before the Team Meeting group themselves.

People should not share someone elses personal matters with others. Gossips and malicious tongues can destroy people and they should not be tolerated in this program! This program is meant to reach out and build up with God's love—not tear down or tear apart with an uncontrolled tongue. Psalm 34:12-13 NKJV says, "Who is the man who desires life, and loves many days, that he may see good? Keep your tongue from evil, and your lips from speaking deceit." James 3:5-6 NKJV says, "Even so the tongue is a little member and boasts great things. See how great a forest a little fire kindles! And the tongue is a fire, a world of iniquity. The tongue is so set among our members that it defiles the whole body, and sets on fire the course of nature; and it is set on fire by hell." James 3:8-10 NKJV continues, "But no man can tame the tongue. It is an unruly evil, full of deadly poison. With it we bless our God and Father, and with it we curse men, who have been made in the similitude of God. Out of the same mouth proceed blessing and cursing. My brethren, these things ought not to be so."

I have put together some ideas of areas that may grow and need to have their own oversight. Depending on the size of the HEART to heart group, one or two people or even a committee can oversee these areas as the group grows.

Each HEART to heart group may want to have a Praise and Worship Team that can lead the members in worshipping the Lord at each of the monthly team meetings. Someone will need to oversee this group and make sure it runs smoothly and is prepared to go at the needed time. The worship and praise team will vary in size and composition. Some groups may have instruments—some may not. Some groups may have more than one song leader—others may not. Each group will be built as God brings people into it.

The HEART to heart group may also want a Kitchen/Serving Team to help set up the fellowship time before each monthly meeting. This team would be established to set up coffee and refreshments before each meeting. They would also be called upon to help cleanup after the meeting. The leader of this group would need to make a schedule for the people to help out. The leader would also need to make arrangments for any coffee, refreshments or kitchen supplies needed at the meeting.

Another group that will probably be needed for oversight will be a Discipleship Support team. This team would assist the small discipleship group leaders in finding out answers to questions about the scriptures and Bible teachings that might come up during the meetings. The people in this group will need to research the question and report back to the small group leader with the answer. This team of overseers would also be on board to check out any Bible Study materials that the group may want to use for discipleship. The group will maintain a list of Bible Studies and books that are approved for use in the small groups. The members of this team would also be responsible for suggesting and listing group members that could qualify as leaders for the small groups. They would also need to interview the prospective group leaders and recommend them to the church leadership for approval.

Another group that may be needed would be a Mentoring and Community Resource team. This team of people would be responsible for putting together a list of community resources that help people in need. As the economy gets bad, more and more people will need assistance with food, bills, gas, clothing, etc. They will also need people who can come to their aid and encourage and lift them up. Some may need to be referred to counselors and others that can help them deal with the tough issues in their lives such as addictions. This team would be responsible for compiling a list of these resources and making it available to the group members and the church leadership. Members on this team would follow up with the people in need to make sure that the need has been addressed. The members of this oversight group may need to periodically go into the community to update their list of resources.

If the HEART to heart group gets large enough, additional people might be needed to help with organization and communication within the group. I would call this the Group Communication and Organization Team.

This group would be responsible for gathering a list of addresses, phone numbers, birthdays, and other pertinent information on the group members. They would also need contact information on the group leaders and to keep track of the small group meeting times and locations. As the group grows and new people come in, they may desire to be included in one of the small groups. This team would be responsible for helping the new person get connected with the small group. This group would also be responsible for keeping track of any special events that the whole HEART to heart team may want to attend. They will also need to track birthdays and other occasions and send out greeting cards to the group members.

The last suggested team of oversight would be the Prayer Team. These people would gather together and pray for each of the HEART to heart groups and their members. They would also be responsible for compiling a list of prayer needs and distributing it to the members at the monthly team meeting. These people would be called upon to pray for the needs of people who desire prayer at the team meeting. They may also want to set up a group prayer chain.

Other leadership groups can be added as the need arises. Each HEART to heart group will have their own needs and they should organize the group to meet those needs. Pastors and others in church leadership can be a valuable resource to help in this area.

One thing to remember is that the more people that get involved in leadership, the more complex that leadership becomes. Each HEART to heart group should keep their leadership as simple as possible. You should only have as many people as it takes to get the job done well. I have included a chart showing the chain of command for the HEART to heart team. You can find it in Appendix A at the back of this book.

I have also put together a proposed agenda for the monthly Team meeting. You can see this proposed agenda in Appendix A. This schedule was set up for a Saturday morning as this is a time when working adults may possibly be able to attend. Weekday mornings don't allow these people the opportunity to participate in the Team Meeting. This schedule can be changed to meet the needs of each HEART to heart group.

It's also important to take time to pray for those in need, whether it is a spiritual or natural need. God knows the best way to meet the needs of the people. Praying will encourage the people, and will move God's hand to work in the lives of those in need.

The first item on the meeting agenda is a brief time of coffee and fellowship. This will give the group members time to get to know each other and allow a 15 minute span of time for those people who always tend to come in late. This will hopefully help eliminate some of the distraction during the rest of the meeting segments.

After the coffee and brief fellowship time, the meeting should begin by welcoming those who come and opening in prayer. Then the group should have a time of praise and worship before the Lord to prepare the hearts for the teaching and Sharing Time. Thanking God for His goodness, mercy, and provision are an integral part of the Christian life. Disciples should honor and worship Jesus. This will also be a place where young Christians can learn how to serve their Lord.

The Beginning/Ice Breaker Activity segment is meant to be an activity that will capture the attention of the group. It should be related to the lesson in some way. It can be a game, object lesson, illustration, or demonstration of something coming up in the Bible teaching. This activity should vary at each meeting so it is fresh and new and will capture the attention of those attending the meeting and point them toward Jesus and/or the upcoming lesson.

After the Beginning/Ice Breaker activity, the Team Leader should present a mini-teaching from the word of God. The teaching should be prepared in a way that will equip the saints and help them learn how to grow as a Christian and begin to reach out to others with their faith. This teaching is the beginning of the process of preparing disciples for service, and keeping them encouraged. Hopefully it will encourage more people to get involved.

Any good foundational Bible basic will work for this teaching time. Lessons prepared from the New Testament would be good because they would teach the group about Jesus, His ministry on earth, and the Christian life. These are great lesson topics for equipping the saints!

After the Bible teaching, the Team Leader should have a short question and answer period to address any questions that may arise from the Bible teaching. These questions are important and should be given attention to insure that the group members understand the lesson. This will help avoid any misinterpretations of items within the teaching. Any questions that cannot be answered should be taken to authority to see if they can help. Once the question is addressed, the answer should be reported back to the group. However, some questions from the Bible simply cannot be answered until we meet Jesus face to face. If this is the case, the teacher should let the group know that the answer cannot be found at this time.

After the question and answer time, the group should take a short break. Pray for the needs of any group members who desire prayer. This will allow for some stretching and a time for those needing to use the bathroom to do so before Sharing Time. This will help reduce the amount of distractions during the presentation time. Also, this will give those doing Sharing Time a few minutes to prepare for their presentation.

Sharing Time is a segment that is open for any group member to bring their gifts and talents and share them with the group. It can also be a time for praise reports, brief testimonies, and teaching of life skills or other things that will help the group members in their daily Christian life. Perhaps someone has a special recipe or a craft they think would benefit the group. Or perhaps someone has a testimony or praise report of something God's done in their life. Or perhaps someone would like to do a cooking class or demonstrate how to care for their car or home. This time is open to all team members who want to participate so long as they abide by the rules and make their presentations in a manner that will help others and glorify God.

In Appendix A, you will find lists of ideas for Sharing Time and mini-classes. These are only ideas, and the list is not limited to these ideas. Be open to suggestions from other team members that can be added to these lists to create a variety of resources for your group. The first list is of ideas that can be finished in one Sharing Time segment. The second list is of possible classes that may take more than one Sharing Time segment to complete. Plan to be open to what interests and edifies the team members. Endeavor to make Sharing Time a blessing to everyone who participates, and encourage the team members to reach out to others and invite them to get involved and get to know each other better. This group can become a place where unbelievers can come and see the love of God in action.

A list of suggested activities for men and one for women will follow the Monthy Team Meeting Schedule. Some of the suggested activity ideas have come from *Women Mentoring Women, Revised Ed.*[3] by Vickie Kraft and Gwynne Johnson (2003, Moody Publishers, Chicago, Illinois, U. S. A., pp. 111-112, 140-142, 175). The ideas borrowed from this resource will be marked with an ** symbol for easy identification.

Sharing Time activities should be planned and approved by leadership before the Team Meeting. This protects the group from any false information and/or destructive activity coming forth during this time. These activities can be nearly any activity that will bless, encourage and build up the group members. Each group member is welcome to bring their ideas for Sharing Time to the meeting and share with others.

After Sharing Time, the Team Leader should close the meeting with prayer. If possible, the meeting should allow a few minutes after Sharing Time for those who want to get more information about the activity to do so. Perhaps someone needs to get a pattern or list of supplies needed for a craft that was demonstrated. Or perhaps someone wants to write down the web site for some great source of information or the ingredients needed for a recipe. Allowing a brief period of fellowship after Sharing Time will help the group members follow up on their questions with the person doing the presentation.

After the meeting, address any questions that may arise, pray for any prayer requests, and make sure everything is resolved and cleaned up. This will help prevent loose ends from falling through the cracks and people getting frustrated because their needs are not being addressed.

If possible, try to stick to the Team Meeting schedule. If for some reason this schedule doesn't work for your group, feel free to make one that does. Whatever schedule you use, try to stick to it. However, if God changes plans on you, be open to listen. Also, at times, special presentations may require changing the routine so it's important to be flexible during these times.

I thank the Lord for each one reading this book, and I will pray that God will bless you as you grow and learn in your Christian walk. I pray that you will have someone to disciple and mentor you during the tough times. We were not meant to be alone to face the giants in our life. God has created us for relationship with Him and with one another. God wants to help us fight the giants in our lives! If we ask Him, He will take them on. With God, all things are possible!

I will also pray that the Lord will raise up people to disciple and mentor those in need. God knows those that are His and whom He has qualified for this necessary task.

Chapter 5

Small Discipleship Groups

Small discipleship groups are the main part of this program. These groups should be the main place where people come to hear the word of God and get encouraged. These groups should be the ones to draw others in to the main part of the plan. The small groups should places where others can go to get ministered to and helped.

Each small group should partake in a Bible study that meets once every one or two weeks. The study should be divided up so that each person spends some time in the word every day on their own. At the end of each week's lesson, the group should meet to discuss it and have some time to fellowship together. Each weekly small group meeting should be a time to talk about those lessons, answer questions, and get to know each other better. These small-group gatherings can be scheduled at the disgression of the group members. These groups should gather in a location where everyone can be comfortable, and the group can have privacy. At times, when God moves on someone's heart, they feel compelled to share personal information with others to get encouragement and support. It is crucial that the group members have privacy, and that they can trust their group members to not gossip and tell others about the things they share.

Small groups can meet in the church, in homes, or in other places in the community. Some community places could include a restaurant, a small business with a Christian owner who may have a break room that could be used, a park, a community hall, a Senior Citizens Center, a grocery store with a delicatesson and a large area of tables and chairs, a coffee house that has an area for people to congregate, etc. Each group that would like to meet in the community should seek out their own special meeting place.

Like the team meetings, I believe each group should be designated either for men or women because the group members will need to have the freedom to speak openly about personal issues. For example, a woman that has been through abuse because of an alcoholic spouse may not feel comfortable speaking in front of other men. Also, a man who may be having physical problems may not feel comfortable talking about them with a group of women. We also need fellowship with those who are the same gender as we are to know that someone else can actually relate to what we are experiencing at the present time. I believe that coed Bible study groups don't provide the freedom to bring up deep heart issues as well as same-gender groups.

The small discipleship groups can also plan special events to do together. They could have a barbeque, picnic, or swimming day after they have their Bible study. They can also have birthday and other holiday parties and do small gift exchanges. They could also implement a "Secret Sister" or "Secret Brother"program as several churches already have set up.

In the "Secret Sister" or "Secret Brother" programs, the group members draw names. Each group member prays for the person whom they drew the name for althrough the next year. The group members also buy a couple small gifts during the year for their secret sister or brother. These can be small gifts to celebrate a birthday, anniversary or other special holiday. Each group member may also want to give their secret sister or brother greeting cards along the way to encourage them in the faith. These little tokens can mean a lot when someone is going through depression, sickness, discouragement, or the death of a friend or family member. It's nice to know that someone cares and that they are praying for you!

Each small group should have a leader who knows the scripture well and lives the Christian life. He or she should also have a passion to share God's word with others and they should be committed. Group leaders should also be reliable, steadfast (for the most part), and be punctual. They need to be an example for those they are discipling. Group leaders should be approved by the church leadership before they begin teaching and mentoring others.

Each small group should be allowed to pick out a Bible study from the Bible or a list of studies that have been approved by the church leadership.

This gives each group some freedom to choose what they would like to study. It would be nice if each study built upon the previous one to teach the group members basic Bible foundations.

As each HEART to heart team grows, they will learn what works and what doesn't work. They will grow in their knowledge of scripture and God will begin using them to minister to others. It's very exciting when the Lord uses you to help touch someone's heart and encourage them. When God moves, people will become more exited about discipling and mentoring others.

During my Christian walk God has allowed me the priviledge of praying the salvation prayer with a few people as they give their hearts to Christ. Nothing touches my heart deeper than knowing God has used me in this way and to help others. There is no earthly pleasure that can ever fulfill my heart's desire more than God using me in this way. You cannot imagine the joy that comes from knowing God has used me to minister to others in ways that truly make a difference!

I pray that each small group will come to know this joy as God moves in and through them.

Chapter 6

Church Authority and Leadership

The fourth component of this discipleship and mentoring plan is the church authority and leadership. These leaders are probably already in established in the church, and they should get honor and respect. They are established by God to help the people of the congregation deal with any issues, scriptural or otherwise, that may arise during the group meetings. These men and women have Godly wisdom, and the HEART to heart groups need to seek Godly counsel and guidance from them in handling certain issues.

Every disciple needs to learn to submit to the church leaders, and trust that they will do their best to help. If you encounter a church leader who is unwilling to help by answering questions or referring you to someone else that can help you, pray for that person. Church leaders are meant to be God's servants and to oversee the church congregation and help keep order and peace.

Jesus has given us authority to make disciples. He has also called and equipped those He desires to be in positions of authority over His people. God knows all things, and sets everything in place so that it will work out His perfect plan as revealed to us in the Holy Bible.

In 1 Timothy 3:1-13 NKJV scripture lays down qualifications for those in church leadership saying, "This is a faithful saying: If a man desires the position of a bishop, he desires a good work. A bishop then must be blameless, the husband of one wife, temperate, sober-minded, of good behavior, hospitable, able to teach; not given to wine, not violent, not greedy for money, but gentle, not quarrelsome, not covetous; one who rules his own home well, having his children in submission with all reverence (for if a man does not know how to rule his own house, how will he take care of the church of God?); not a novice, lest being puffed up with pride he fall into the same condemnation as the devil. Moreover he must have a good testimony among those who are outside, lest he fall into reproach and the snare of the devil. Likewise deacons must be reverent, not double-tongued, not given to much wine, not greedy for money, holding the mystery of the faith with a pure conscience. But let these also first be tested, then let them serve as deacons, being found blameless. Likewise, their wives must be reverent, not slanderers, temperate, faithful in all things. Let deacons be the husbands of one wife, ruling their children and their own homes well. For those who have served well as deacons obtain for themselves a good standing and great boldness in the faith which is in Christ Jesus."

Church leadership should be examples for the rest of the people. They should lead the people toward Christ and watch out over them. They are put in authority positions to serve those in the body of Christ.

As you establish procedures for your discipleship and mentoring groups, you should always consult the church leadership and get their advice on how to set up your group. Church leaders, such as Pastors and Elders, have a lot of experience and wisdom in dealing with people. They are a great resource that God has provided for members of each church congregation.

Scripture tells us to honor our elders saying, "Let the elders who rule well be counted worthy of double honor, especially those who labor in the word and doctrine." (1 Timothy 5:17 NKJV)

Chapter 7

Choosing Group Leaders

Group leaders for any of the discipleship groups should be approved by the leadership. These people should have the same desires and heart as those in leadership—to be holy and blameless in the sight of God and others and to be an example for others in following Jesus. They should also have a passion for God's word and for serving others.

Jesus, when questioned by the mother of the sons of Zebedee, said, "(...) You know that the rulers of the Gentiles lord it over them, and those who are great exercise authority over them. Yet it shall not be so among you; but whoever desires to become great among you, let him be your servant. And whoever desires to be first among you, let him be your slave—just as the Son of Man did not come to be served, but to serve, and to give His life a ransom for many." (Matthew 20:25-28 NKJV)

Scripture also says, "Let no one despise your youth, but be an example to the believers in word, in conduct, in love, in spirit, in faith, in purity. Till I come give attention to reading, to exhortation, to doctrine. Do not neglect the gift that is in you, which was given to you by prophesy, with the laying on of the hands of the eldership. Meditate on these things; give yourself entirely to them, that your progress may be evident to all. Take heed to yourself and to the doctrine. Continue in them, for in doing this you will save both yourself and those who hear you." (1 Timothy 4:12-16 NKJV) This scripture presents a picture of the type of person needed for the leadership over a HEART to heart Discipleship and Mentoring group.

Though the person is not yet perfected, they press on towards the goal of what Christ has for them.

Anyone wanting to disciple others should believe and be in agreement with scripture and the Statement of Faith of the church doing this plan. They must also be approved by leadership beforehand. Without this agreement, unexpected disputes over doctrine could cause friction between people in the group resulting in unwanted division.

One way of approaching the challenge of choosing those who can disciple others is to put together a list of requirements to be met by those who wish to disciple small groups in the church. Some of these requirements might include a certain number of years of service in a ministry, a basic foundational knowledge of the Bible, being born again by the Holy Spirit, and being a example of someone who is trying to live according to the truth in God's Word. After compiling the list of requirements, set up an interview process and interview each person. Then send a list of prospective discipleship group leaders to the elders or church leadership for their approval. Once that person is approved, the Team Leadership should help them establish a group to disciple.

In scripture, Jesus gives us the authority to make disciples of all nations. In Matthew 28:18-20 NKJV scripture tells us, "And Jesus came and spoke to them, saying, 'All authority has been given to Me in heaven and on earth. Go therefore and make disciples of all the nations, baptizing them in the name of the Father and of the Son and of the Holy Spirit, teaching them to observe all things that I have commanded you; and lo, I am with you always, even to the end of the age." Amen.

Chapter 8

Choosing Discipleship Materials

I would begin my discipleship teachings with materials that teach the group members about being a disciple and discipling others. There are several ways to learn about disciples and discipleship. The best way is to look up all the Bible verses that speak of disciples and discipleship, and as you locate each verse, make notes about the message the verse is giving. Each verse should add a little more to the meaning of discipleship, and help understand it better.

As you begin your discipleship training, it's good to invest in a study Bible. The Bible you choose should be a mainstream Bible which means that it has been organized and put together by a large group of scholars from a variety of different Christian denominations. Bibles that are made and printed by one company for a specific denomination or group of people may not be accurate. They may have been altered to fit a specific teaching.

The reason I suggest a study Bible is because it has a variety of notes and information that help explain the meaning of the scripture. Sometimes it's difficult to understand what the scripture is talking about. These study notes can help you understand. Also, a study Bible has maps and other helps to give you more information about the places and customs of the people that were living in Bible times. Also, most Bibles have a concordance in the back that helps you locate specific Bible verses if you know a word that is in the verse. Concordances make locating specific scripture much easier.

Another tool that a Bible student might want to invest in is a good Bible dictionary. These dictionaries help define terms in the Bible so that you can understand them better. At times Bible study books will use a lot of large words, and for new Bible students it may be hard to understand. The dictionary will be a good investment.

Another way to learn about discipleship is to read Christian books on the topic. At times, others' insight can add to our learning. We should be careful that the people giving us this insight are telling the truth by checking to see that what they tell us is in agreement with scripture.

I would suggest that a beginning Bible student start reading in the book of Matthew and work through the New Testament. The New Testament begins with the Gospels (Matthew, Mark, Luke, John) and that is where you can learn about Jesus and His disciples. As you learn about Jesus and His disciples, you will begin to what the HEART to heart Discipleship and Mentoring program is about. You will also see what is involved in becoming a disciple of Christ. You will also see how Jesus went about calling and teaching His disciples, and you will learn about the miracles Jesus did during His ministry on earth. You will get a glimpse of how the Master worked and how he did only the Father's will.

Also, any good, foundational Bible study that teaches about Jesus and His disciples would work for the teaching part of this program. There are many resources available in the form of small group Bible Studies. If you are a new Christian believer, it might be wise to have a pastor or someone who has been a Christian for a long time help pick out Bible studies for you to use.

To avoid heresy, all of the materials used in this program should be approved by the church leadership before the teaching begins. There are many false teachers spreading a variety of mistaken ideas to any Christian that doesn't know scripture well enough to know that they are mistaken. By having the authority approve study materials before they are used, hopefully, you can avoid most of this confusion.

Chapter 9

Bringing it all Together

Now that we've covered the basics of the HEART to heart Discipleship and Mentoring Plan, we must look at what is involved in bringing it all together. Putting a group like this together requires a great deal of prayer and preparation. A person who is thinking about starting a program like this must spend time in prayer and seek God for His will. Without God, this plan will be fruitless and those who work at putting the program together will be doing so without having the power and presence of God with them in it. As a result, the program will not have the impact or the fruit that it should produce.

The person starting this program up should pray for God's direction and wisdom. They should also pray that He will bring in the people He wants to organize, teach, and learn from the program, and that God will show you where each person should be placed in the team. As that person continues to seek God, he will know how to proceed.

As you pray, seek counsel, and share the program plan with others, people may come on board to help get the program started. This program is too much for one person to take on by themselves. It requires of team of dedicated people who believe in Jesus Christ and what this program is doing. It requires a team of people who will be willing to committ to doing the hard work to get it started and keep it going. Discipleship is not a program for fair-weather friends. The people involved need to be committed and to endure and persevere through the tough times.

I know Satan, the enemy of our souls, hates anyone or anything that promotes God. Therefore, we can know He will come against those who try to start a discipleship and mentoring program. He wants God's children to fail, fall, and be eliminated. He just doesn't know that God has already won the victory for His children, and Satan can never succeed against God or His children. God will do battle for us as we battle against principalities and powers in the dark spiritual realms. They do not want God glorified on earth!

I know the prospect of spiritual battle is not something that we desire to have to do. However, I don't want to present this program as something that will be easy to do. That would be a lie and would leave a lot of fellow believers disillusioned. I want to be honest and let you know that in doing this you may face a tough spiritual battle. However, if you give the battle to God, stand firm, and persevere through it—you will bring glory and pleasure to God!

Appendix A

Chart 1: Chain of Authority

God (Father, Son-Jesus, Holy Spirit)
↓
Elders*/Pastor
↓
Deacons
↓
Team Leader
↓
Team Leadership Groups
↓
Small Group Leaders
↓
Group Members

**Note: Some churches have different names for their leaders such as Deacons, Bishops, etc. If your leadership are called by different titles, you may want to verify your chain of command.

Chart 2: Monthly Team Meeting Agenda

9:00-9:15 a.m.	Coffee and Fellowship Time (Possibly with fruit or pastry)
9:15-9:20 a.m.	Welcome the people; Introduce new people
9:20-9:30 a.m.	Open in prayer
9:30-9:50 a.m.	Worship the Lord
9:50-10:00 a.m.	Beginning/Ice Breaker Activity
10:00-10:45 a.m.	Bible Study Time: Begin with training on Becoming a Disciple and Discipleship
10:45-10:55 a.m.	Question and Answer Session
10:55-11:05 a.m.	Short break/Individual Prayer Time
11:05-11:30 a.m.	Sharing Time *
11:30-11:35 a.m.	Closing Prayer
11:35-11:45 a.m.	Final Questions/Cleanup

*A time of sharing and teaching things that pertain to the age and gender of those in the group. All those wanting to share with the group are invited to come and participate.

Chart 3: Sharing Time Ideas for Women

Praise Reports

Share Born Again Experiences

Guest Speakers from
Christian Organizations

Interior Design

Skits / Drama

Stress Management

Special Music

Art Demonstrations

Mission Outreaches

Craft Demonstrations

Aerobics**/Exercises

Special Holiday Meals

Cultures & Customs of Other
Lands

Tutoring

Microwave Cooking**

Cooking on a Low-Budget

Weight Management**

Encouraging: Ideas to Lift Up
Others

Testimonies

First Aid

Sharing Spiritual Gifts

Cooking
Demonstrations

Ideas for enhancing marriages

Poetry/Short Stories

Platform for trying out
Ministry

Ideas for Children's Activities

Hospitality, Manners

Cake Decorating**

Home Schooling

Easy One Dish Meals

Legal Matter Chatter**

Do the Most with What You
Have**

Choosing Healthy Food

Coping With Codependency**

Desktop Publishing
Caring for the Aged
Discipline Ideas for Children
Entertainment for Children
Teaching Children
Responsibility (Chores)
Making a Cookbook
Abortion—Not a Choice
Being a Good Citizen
Abuse/Divorce/Recovery
Recovering From Substance
Abuse
Dessert/Fellowship Time
Sharing short stories/poems
Tips for Home Cleaning
Scrapbooking
Making Greeting Cards
Sewing

Issues for Working Women**

Holiday Home Decor
Scrapbook Pages
Letter Writing

Support for Singles
Church Library
Abortion Recovery
Living Trust Funds
Helping the Homeless

Supporting Widows
Tips for organization
Tips for making gifts
Rubber Stamping**
Photography
Needlecrafts

**Ideas from Women Mentoring Women, Revised Edition, (Kraft, Vickie and Johnson, Gwynne, 2003)

Chart 4: Sharing Time Classes for Women

Nutrition

Writing

Computer

Photography

Decorating ideas for a low budget

Quilting**

Knitting**

Cross Stitch**

Restoring Used Items

Childcare

Homecare

Beading

Nature Crafts

Gift Ideas

Household Tips

Stocking a Pantry

Food Safety

Home Safety

Sculpture

Organization Tips

House Keeping

Budgeting

Family History

Scrapbooking

Drawing

Sewing/mending

Cartooning

Crochet

Applique

Parenting

Clothing Repair

Gardening

Make Stepping Stones

Card Making

Mosaics

Menu Planning

Sculpture

Community Safety

Painting

Day Planner

Track your Checkbook

Recipes

Exercises

Clothing Care

Soap Making

Stenciling**

Flower Arranging**

Christmas Crafts

Rubber Stamping**

Child Birth

Choosing Clothing

Email your Friends

Caring for Your Pet

Ideas to Simplify Life

Taming Your Teenagers

Dare to Discipline

Holiday Decorating Ideas

One Pot Meals

Spicing It Up!

Create Your Resume

Bread Making

Candle Making

Hygiene

Calligraphy

Candy Making

Cover it With Fabric**

Prayer

Cooking

Creating a Resume

Paper Crafts

Become a Pen Pal

Choices and

Consequences

Baking

Put Christ into your

Holiday

Making Special

Moments

**Ideas from Women Mentoring Women, Rev. Edition, (Kraft, Vickie and Johnson, Gwynne, 2003)

Chart 5: Sharing Time Ideas for Men

Praise Reports

Share Born Again Experiences

Guest Speakers from Christian Organizations

Woodworking Demonstrations

Skits / Drama

Special Music

Using Basic Tools

Outdoor Grilling

Home Finances

Aerobics**/Exercises

Making Memories

Cultures & Customs of Other Lands

Tutoring

Microwave Cooking**

Cooking on a Low-Budget

Mission Updates

Weight Management**

Testimonies

First Aid

Sharing Spiritual Gifts

Basic Home Repair

Cooking

Ideas for enhancing marriages**

Sharing Short Stories

Platform for trying out Ministry

Basic Car Care

Hospitality, Manners

Repairs

Home Schooling

Easy One Dish Meals

Legal Matter Chatter**

Do the Most with What You Have**

Choosing Healthy Food

Encouraging—Ideas to Lift Up Others

Travel Experiences

Desktop Publishing

Caring for the Aged

Dealing with Anger

Gifts You Can Make

Teaching Children Responsibility (Chores)

Leading your Family

Abortion—Not a Choice

Being a Good Citizen

Abuse/Divorce Recovery

Recovering From Substance Abuse

Dessert/Fellowship Time

Tips for Home Cleaning

Hunting and Fishing Tips

Basic Clothing Repair

Mediation Strategies

Missions

Organizing your shop

Fostering Family Relationships

Coping With Codependency**

Issues for Working Men

Disciplining Children

Entertainment for Children

Letter Writing

Support for Singles

Church Library

Abortion Recovery

Taming Teenagers

Helping the Homeless

Confrontation

Gift Ideas for others

Photography

Peace Making

Power Tool Tips

Choices and Consequences

Family Ministry Ideas

**Ideas from Women Mentoring Women, Rev. Ed., (Kraft, Vickie and Johnson, Gwynne, 2003)

Chart 6: Sharing Time Classes for Men

Nutrition	Budgeting
Writing	Hygiene
Computer	Photography
Clothing Repair	Restoring Used Items
Parenting	Childcare
Homecare	Gardening
Lawn Care	Raising Boys
Nature Crafts	Gift Ideas
Woodworking	
Household Tips	Easy Home Repairs
Hunters Safety	
Food Safety	Community Safety
Home Safety	
Day Planner	Organization Tips
Fishing Tips	
House Keeping	Easy Recipes
Exercises	
Clothing Care	Cooking on the Grill
Power Tools	
Prayer	Child Birth
Cooking	
Choosing Clothing	Creating a Resume

Email your Friends

Become a Pen Pal

Ideas to Simplify Life

Dare to Discipline

Put Christ into your Holiday

Making Special Moments

Baking Lessons

Family

Ministry Ideas

Family Problem Solving

Subtance Abuse Recovery

Peace Making

Writing a Resume

Caring for Your Pet

Basic Car Care

Choices/ Consequences

Anger Management

Spice It Up!

One Pot Meals

Taming Your Teenagers

Other Cultures

Money Management

Family Priorities

Outreach Ideas

Work Skills Classes

**Ideas from Women Mentoring Women, Revised Ed., (Kraft, Vickie and Johnson, Gwynne, 2003)

Reproducibles

The last section of this guidebook for the HEART to heart Discipleship and Mentoring Plan is a section of resources that you can photocopy and use for your church's Discipleship and Mentoring Program. These are basic tools to help with recordkkeeping and promotion. Feel free to alter them to meet your needs.

My heart will be in prayer for those who desire to let God use them in a HEART to heart Discipleship and Mentoring Program in their church. I pray that He will pour His love into our hearts and help us learn to love Him back and love others as He has commanded us to do. I will pray that God will accomplish all He desires through each one of us. He has the power to accomplish great works!

May God be with you as you endeavor to disciple and mentor others with this plan. To Him be the glory for all that is accomplished!

Below is a list of the reproducible items you can use for your congregation:

1. Letter of Inquiry (to find out if there is an interest in Discipling in your congregation
2. Congregational Survey Form
3. Flyer
4. Membership List
5. Member Information Sheet
6. Team Meeting Member Attendance Chart
7. Communication Card

Date:

Dear Brothers and Sisters in Christ,

Our church is presently considering starting up a HEART to heart Discipleship and Mentoring program. We are excited about the possibility of training up disciples and mentoring those who need encouragement and help during difficult times in their lives.

We are sending out letters to each member of our congregation to find out if they would be interested in a Discipleship and Mentoring program. We would love to hear from you about this matter.

Enclosed is a postcard with a brief survey for you to fill out and return to the church office. Please answer the questions and return the survey at your earliest convenience. If you have any questions, you can contact the church office.

Sincerely,

Congregational Survey Form

Name:_____Phone_____

Address:_____

Would you be interested in joining a Discipleship and Mentoring group in your area?

_____

Would you be interested in helping others deal with tough issues in their lives?

_____

Would you be interested in sharing God's word with others in a small group setting?

_____

Would you be interested in helping organize a discipleship and mentoring group?

_____

Would you like to learn about God's word?
Would you like to learn more about discipleship?
Would you like to help others work through their problems?
If so, come and join our

HEART to heart
Discipleship & Mentoring
Program

Come and let the Love of God work in your heart and life!

Who: When:

Where: Cost:

For more information contact:

HEART to heart Membership List

Name: Phone No.

_____

_____

_____

_____

_____

_____

_____

_____

_____

_____

_____

_____

_____

_____

_____

_____

_____

_____

_____

_____

_____

_____

_____

HEART to heart Member Information Sheet

Name: _____

Phone No._____

Address: _____

Email Address: _____

Prayer Needs: _____

Hobbies: _____

Small group assignment: _____

Is this member a teacher or leader? _____

If so, which group do they teach/lead? _____

Date they became a member: _____

Do they belong to this church? _____

If not, which church do they attend?_____

Favorite Color: _____

Birthday: _____

Anniversary:_____

Team Meeting Yearly Attendance Chart

Name: _____

Phone No._____

Address: _____

Jan. _____ Feb. _____ March _____ April _____

May _____ June _____ July _____ Aug. _____

Sept. _____ Oct. _____ Nov. _____ Dec. _____

Place a check mark in each box when the member attends the monthly meeting.

Team Meeting Yearly Attendance Chart

Name: _____

Phone No._____

Address: _____

Jan. _____ Feb. _____ March _____ April _____

May _____ June _____ July _____ Aug. _____

Sept. _____ Oct. _____ Nov. _____ Dec. _____

Place a check mark in each box when the member attends the monthly meeting.

HEART to heart
Communication Card

Name: _____ Phone No._____

Address: _____

Email:_____

I am a _____ regular member _____ guest _____ visitor

I heart about the HEART to heart program from:

_____

_____

I am interested in: _____ more information about HEART to heart

_____information about the church   _____prayer

_____mentoring _____discipleship_____other

If you chose other, please explain:

_____

Please pray for:

_____

End Notes

1. Women Mentoring Women, Rev. Ed., by Vicky Kraft and Gwynne Johnson, (2003), Moody Publishers, Chicago, Illinois, U. S. A.

2. NKJV Study Bible, 2nd Edition, Thomas Nelson Publishers, Nashville, Tennessee, U. S. A.

3. Ibid. Women Mentoring Women.